Put Beginning Readers on the Right Track with
ALL ABOARD READING™

The All Aboard Reading series is especially for beginning readers. Written by noted authors and illustrated in full color, these are books that children really and truly *want* to read—books to excite their imagination, tickle their funny bone, expand their interests, and support their feelings. With five different reading levels, All Aboard Reading lets you choose which books are most appropriate for your children and their growing abilities.

Picture Readers—for Ages 3 to 6
Picture Readers have super-simple texts, with many nouns appearing as rebus pictures. At the end of each book are 24 flash cards—on one side is the rebus picture; on the other side is the written-out word.

Pre-Level 1—for Ages 4 to 6
First Friends, First Readers have a super-simple text starring lovable recurring characters. Each book features two easy stories that will hold the attention of even the youngest reader while promoting an early sense of accomplishment.

Level 1—for Preschool through First-Grade Children
Level 1 books have very few lines per page, very large type, easy words, lots of repetition, and pictures with visual "cues" to help children figure out the words on the page.

Level 2—for First-Grade to Third-Grade Children
Level 2 books are printed in slightly smaller type than Level 1 books. The stories are more complex, but there is still lots of repetition in the text, and many pictures. The sentences are quite simple and are broken up into short lines to make reading easier.

Level 3—for Second-Grade through Third-Grade Children
Level 3 books have considerably longer texts, harder words, and more complicated sentences.

All Aboard for happy reading!

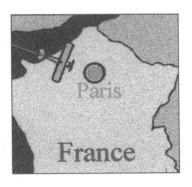

To Kellon - equal to any challenge—S.A.K

Photo credits: p. 7, Corbis; p. 12-13, Bettman / Corbis; p. 46-47, Bettman / Corbis

Library of Congress Cataloging-in-Publication Data is available.

ISBN 0-448-42634-X (pb)   A B C D E F G H I J
ISBN 0-448-42666-8 (GB)   A B C D E F G H I J

ALL
ABOARD
READING™

Level 2
Grades 1-3

NIGHT FLIGHT

Charles Lindbergh's Incredible Adventure

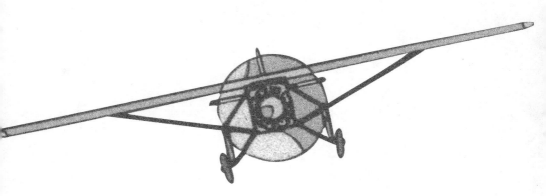

By S.A. Kramer
Illustrated by Dan Andreasen

Grosset & Dunlap • New York

May 20, 1927

It is early morning
on Long Island, New York.
A handsome young pilot heads
toward his plane.

It is not a good day for flying.

A light rain is falling.

Fog drifts through the air.

But he gets in his plane.

He buckles his seat belt.

He puts on his helmet.

Down come his goggles.

The pilot is named

Charles Lindbergh.

He wants to make

the most daring flight ever.

And bad weather

will not stop him.

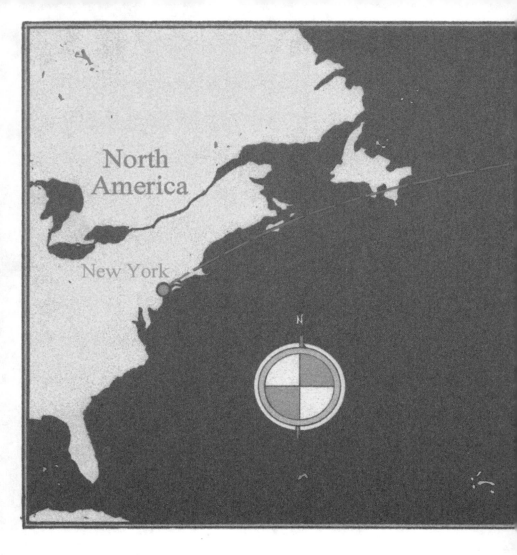

Charles wants to fly

from New York to Paris

without a stop.

No one has done it before.

Six men have died trying.

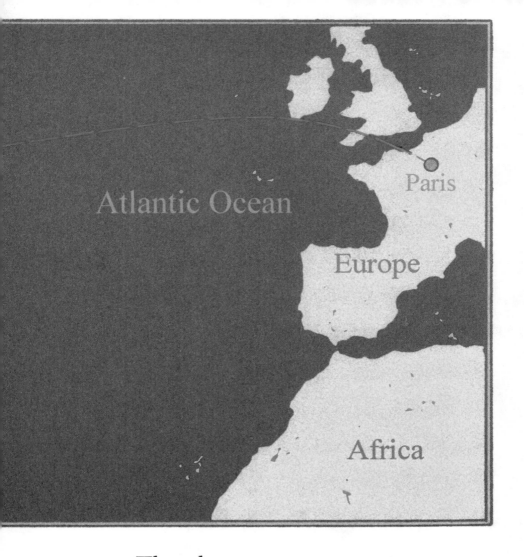

The plane can go

only 100 miles an hour.

So the trip will take

nearly a day and a half.

Hardly anyone thinks

he can make it.

Charles is only 25 years old.

He has not been

a pilot for long.

And he is making the trip

all alone.

Newspapers call him

the flying fool.

His plane is tiny.

It has just one engine.

There is no window.

The gas tank is in front.

The only way to see

is to lean out the side.

The cockpit only has room

for a chair.

Charles can't even stretch

his legs.

Newspapers call it

a flying coffin.

There is hardly anything on board—

no radio to call for help

and no parachute.

He has only five sandwiches,

and two canteens of water.

Charles wants to keep the plane
as light as possible.
It needs nearly 3,000 pounds
of gas to get to Paris.
All that gas makes the plane
heavy and slow.

It may not even get off the ground.

But Charles believes in his plane.

And he believes in himself.

It is now nearly eight o'clock.

This is the moment.

The engine roars.

The propeller spins.

The plane starts down the runway.

The plane heads up—

and comes down.

It goes up again.

Then down it plops.

Then suddenly it lifts

toward the sky!

Charles clears some phone lines

by only twenty feet.

His great adventure has begun.

Up in the gray sky,

Charles is all alone.

He is heading to Canada.

Then he will cross the ocean.

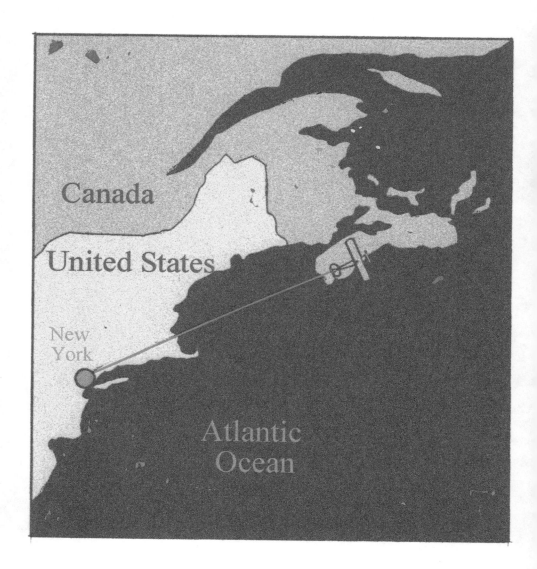

It is cool in the plane.

But his flying suit

keeps him warm.

Suddenly the sun bursts out.

Now it is boiling hot inside.

Charles will just have to sweat.

There is no room

to take his suit off.

The sun is not out for long.

Over Canada,

storm clouds gather.

By early afternoon,

Rain sweeps into the cockpit.

Charles is not hot anymore.

Now he is cold and wet.

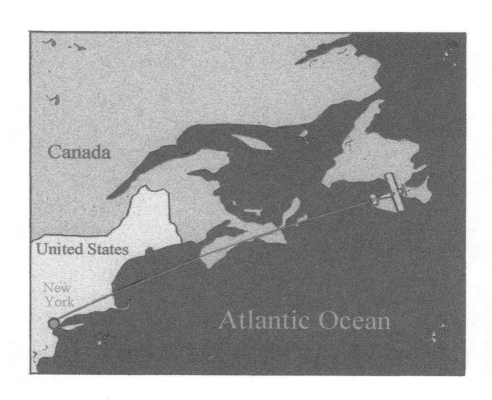

The hours drag by.

Canada is still below.

Charles feels like

he has been flying forever.

But it is only four o'clock.

He is stiff from sitting.

His eyes hurt.

And he is getting bored—

bored and sleepy.

So Charles talks to himself.

He must stay awake.

If he nods off,

he might crash or get lost.

Night begins to fall.

It is 12 hours

since takeoff.

Charles longs to go to bed.

But he will not turn back.

He would rather die than fail.

Now it is time to cross the ocean.

Darkness spreads over the waves.

Below him are icebergs.

Ahead rolls thick fog.

Up in the cockpit,

Charles is the loneliest person

in the world.

The night is cold.

Charles shivers in his seat.

His feet start to freeze.

Suddenly a storm strikes!

Hail and sleet

hammer the plane.

It is so cold,

his compass stops working.

Charles turns on his flashlight.

Oh, no!

He sees ice on the wings.

That can make a plane crash!

Charles is in trouble.

But he keeps his head.

He flies lower

where the air is warmer.

The warm air will melt the ice.

The wind whips the plane

like a feather.

He is right above the water.

The ice disappears.

The storm breaks up.

Charles is safe!

Now the moon glows brightly.

The stars shine on Charles.

But he is so tired,

he cannot stop his eyes

from closing.

Charles shakes himself all over.

He slaps his face hard.

He is now halfway to Paris.

But how, he wonders, can he go on?

Charles makes the plane dive.

Then he jerks it up to the clouds.

Anything to stay awake.

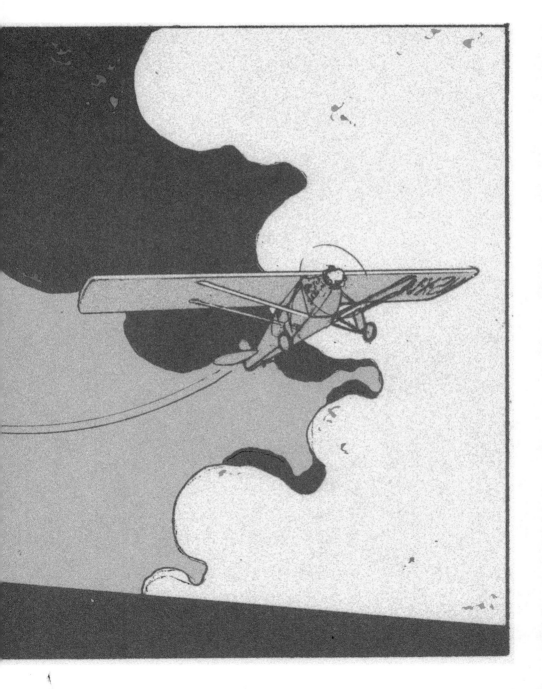

It is morning again.

Charles is so sleepy,

he cannot think.

He has been flying

for nearly 24 hours.

But thick fog is all around.

Rain sloshes into the cockpit.

He is flying blind!

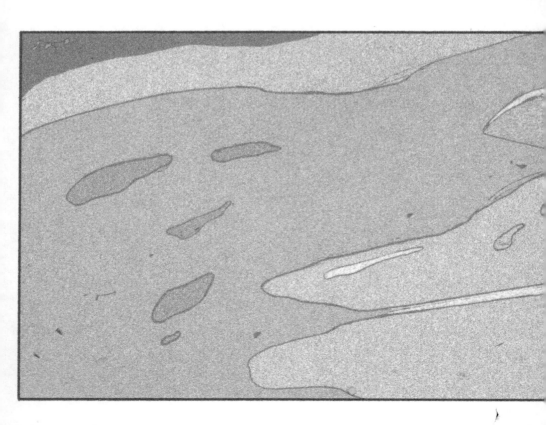

Strange shapes float behind him.

They have voices.

And they tell him how to fly.

Are they ghosts?

Or is he so tired that

he is imagining things?

The fog slowly lifts.

Is that a porpoise in the water?

Is that a gull flying by?

Yes!

Fishing boats bob on the waves.

Charles shouts out,

"Which way is Ireland?"

No one answers.

But it does not matter.

Ahead lie the cliffs

and the green fields of Ireland.

Charles can see people running

and cheering him on.

Land!

Now Charles is wide awake.

The six hours to Paris zoom by.

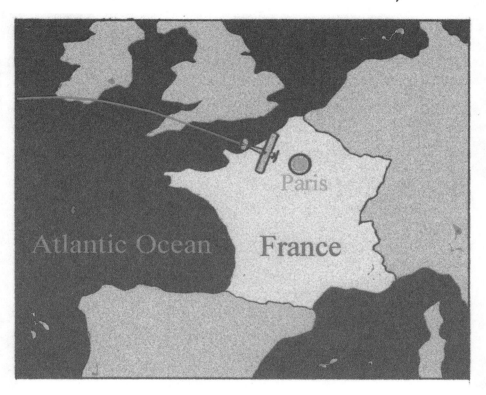

Flying is easy.

The plane feels like part

of his body.

It is night

when he reaches the city.

The airfield is below!

After $33\frac{1}{2}$ hours and 3,614 miles,

Charles has made history!

But all he can think about

is taking a nap.

At 10:24 P.M.,

Charles touches down.

Over 100,000 people are waiting.

As the plane stops,

they burst toward him.

They shout his name.

Everyone wants to see

the young hero.

Overnight,

Charles has become the most famous

man on earth.

All over the world,

people celebrate.

In New York,

they kiss and hug.

They toss confetti out windows.

Boats blow their horns.

Fire engines pull their sirens.

All over America,

church bells ring.

Now thousands of people fly across
the ocean every day.
But it all started
with one person—
Charles Lindbergh.